NUMBER 396

THE ENGLISH
EXPERIENCE

ITS RECORD IN EARLY PRINTED BOOKS
PUBLISHED IN FACSIMILE

WILLIAM LAUD

A SPEECH CONCERNING
INNOVATIONS
IN THE CHURCH

LONDON 1637

DA CAPO PRESS
THEATRVM ORBIS TERRARVM LTD.
AMSTERDAM 1971 NEW YORK

The publishers acknowledge their gratitude
to the Syndics of Cambridge University Library
for their permission to reproduce
the Library's copy (Shelfmark: Syn.7.63.245)
and to the Curators of the Bodleian Library, Oxford
for their permission to reproduce
the pages from the Library's copies
(Shelfmarks: 4.0.79.Th.13 and Douce TT 164)

Library of Congress Catalog Card Number:
79-171771

S.T.C. No. 15306

Collation: A^4, a^4, B-L^4

Published in 1971 by

Theatrum Orbis Terrarum Ltd.,

O.Z. Voorburgwal 85, Amsterdam

&

Da Capo Press

- a division of Plenum Publishing Corporation -

227 West 17th Street, New York, 10011

Printed in the Netherlands

ISBN 90 221 0396 x

1618449

A SPEECH

DELIVERED IN THE
STARR-CHAMBER,
ON WEDNESDAY, THE
XIVth of IUNE, MDCXXXVII.

AT THE CENSVRE,
Of ⎰ Iohn Bastwick,
⎱ Henry Burton, &
⎱ William Prinn;
Concerning pretended *Innovations*
In the CHURCH.

By the most Reverend Father in GOD,
WILLIAM,
L. Archbishop of *Canterbury* his *Grace*.

LONDON,
Printed by RICHARD BADGER,
MDCXXXVII.

TO
HIS MOST
SACRED MAJESTIE,
CHARLES,
BY THE GRACE OF GOD,

King of Great Brittaine, France *and* Ireland,
Defender *of the* Faith, *&c.*

Moſt Gracious, and Dread Soveraigre;

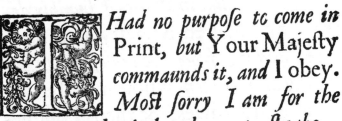 *Had no purpoſe to come in* Print, *but* Your Majeſty *commaunds it, and* I obey. *Moſt ſorry* I am *for the* Occaſion, *that induced mee to ſpeake, and that ſince hath moved* You *to command mee to* Print. *Nor am* I ignorant that many things, while they are ſpoken*

A 3   *ſpoken*

spoken and paffe by the Eare *but once, give* *great content;* which when they come to the Eyes of men, and their often *fcan-* *ning, may lye open to fome* exceptions. *This may fall to my* lot *in this particular,* and very eafily, confidering my many *di-* verfions, *and the little time f could fnatch* *from other* Imployment *to attend* this. *Yet choofe f rather to* obey Your Maje- fty, *than to* facrifice *to mine owne* priva- cy and content.

Since then this Speech *uttered in pub-* like, in the Star-chamber, *muft now come* *to be more publike in* Print; *f humbly de-* fire Your Sacred Maiefty *to* protect mee, *and* it, *from the undeferved* Ca- lumny *of thofe men,* whofe mouthes are fpears and arrowes, & their Tongues
Pfal.57.4. a fharpe fword. *Pfal.*57. *Though as the* wifeman *fpeakes,* their foolifh mouthes have already called for their owne
ftripes,

ftripes, and their lippes (*and pennes*) been a fnare for their foules, *Prov*.18. Prov.18.6,7
The Occafion *which led mee to this* Speech *is knowne. There have of late beene divers* Libells *fpread againft the* Prelates *of this* Church. *And they have not beene more* bitter, *which is the* fhame *of thefe* raging waves, *than they are ut-* Jude ver.13. *terly* falfe, *which is* Our happinefs. *But I muft humbly befeech* Your Maiefty *to confider, that 'tis not Wee onely, that is, the* Bifhops, *that are ftrucke at, but through our fides,* Your Majefty, Your Honor, Your Safety, Your Religion, *is impea-ched. For what* fafety *can You expect, if You loofe the hearts of Your* people ? *And how can You retaine their* hearts, *if You change their* Religion *into* fuperftition ? *And what* Honour *can You hope for, either* Prefent, *or derivative to* Pofterity *if you attend your* Government *no better*
then

then to suffer Your Prelates *to put this* change *upon You?* And what Majesty *can any* Prince *retaine, if hee loose his* Honour *and his* People?

G o d *be thanked* 'T *is in all points o-therwise with You:* For God *hath blessed You with a* Religious *heart, & not subject to* change. And He hath filled You with Honor *in the* Eyes *of Your* People: *And by their* Love *and dutifulnesse, He hath made You* safe. So that Your Maiesty *is upheld and Your* Crowne *flourishing in the* Eyes *of* Christendome. And God *forbid any* Libellous *blast at home from the* Tongues *or* Pennes *of a few, should* shrivell *up any growth of these.*

Wee *have received, and daily doe re-ceive from* G o d, *many and great* Bles-sings *by* You. And I *hope they are not many that are* unthankfull *to* You, *or to* God *for You.* And that there should bee
none

none in a Populous Nation, *even* Ene-
mies *to their owne* happineſſe, *cannot bee
expected. Yet Ꝯ ſhall deſire, even theſe to
call themſelves to an account, and to remember, that* Blaſphemy *againſt* God,
and ſlandering the footſteps of his An-
nointed *are joined together,* Pſal. Pſalm. 89. ver. 50.
89. *For he that* blaſphemes God, Wherewith thine E-
nemies have blaſphe-
will never ſticke at the ſlander *of* med Thee, and ſlan-
dered the footſteppes
his Prince; *And he that gives him-* of thine Ancinted,
ſelfe the Liberty *to* ſlander *his* Prince,
will quickly aſcend to the next higheſt,
and Blaſpheme God.

But then, as Ꝯ deſire them *to remember, ſo I doe moſt humbly beſeech* your
Maieſty *to account with Your ſelfe too:
And not to meaſure your* peoples love
by the unworthineſſe of thoſe few. For a
loyall *and obedient* people *You have, and
ſuch as will ſpare nor* Livelyhood, *nor*
a Life,

Life *to doe You* ſervice : *And are joyed at*
the heart to ſee the Moderation *of your*
Government *and your* conſtancy *to*
maintaine Religion, *and your* Piety *in*
Exampling *it.*

And as I *thus* beſeech You *for Your*
People *in* generall, *ſo doe* I particularly
for the three Profeſsions *which have a*
little ſuffer'd in theſe three *moſt* Noto -
rious Libellers Perſons.

And firſt for my *owne* Profeſsion, *J*
humbly begge of your Majeſty *to thinke*
M. Burton *hath not in this many fol-*
lowers, and am heartily ſorry hee would
needs lead. *The beſt is,* your Majeſty
knows what made his Rancour *ſwell; Jle*
ſay no more.

And for the Law, *J truly* honor *it*
with my heart, and believe Mr. Prynn
may ſeeke all the Innes of Court, *(and*
with

with a Candle *too if he will*) *and scarce find such a* Malevolent *as himselfe a-gainst* State *and* Church. *And because* hee hath so frequently thrust mistaken Law *into these* Pamphlets, *to wrong the* Governors *of the* Church, *and a-buse your good and well-minded* people, *and makes* Burton *and* Baftwick *utter* Law *which, God knowes, they under-stand not, (for I doubt his Pen is in all the* Pamphlets,) *J doe humbly in the* Churches *name desire of your* Maje-ftie, *that it may be* resolved *by all the* Reverend Iudges *of* ENGLAND, *and then* publifhed *by your* Majefty, *That our keeping* Courts, *and issuing* Pro-ceffe *in our owne* Names, *and the like* Exceptions *formerly taken, and now renewed, are not against the* Lawes *of the* Realme, *(as 'tis most certaine they*

are

are not) *That so the* Church-Governors *may goe on cheerfully in their* duetie, *and the peoples minds be* quieted *by this Assurance, that neither the* Law, *nor their* Libertie, *as* Subjects, *is therby infringed*.

And for Physicke, *the* Profession *is* honourable, *and safe; and I know the* Professors *of it will remember that* Corpus humanum, *mans body,is that, about which their Art is conversant, not* Corpus Ecclesiasticum,*or* Politicum, *the Body of the* Church, *State, or Common-wealth*. Bastwick *onely hath been bold that way. But the* Proverbe *in the* Gospell, *in the fourth of* S. Luke *is all I'le say to him*, Medice, cura teipsum, *Physician heale thy selfe. And yet let me tell* your Majestie, *I believe hee hath gained more by making the*
Church

S. Luke, 4. 23.

Church a Patient, *than by all the*
Patients *hee ever had beside.*

Sir, *both* my felfe, *and my* Brethren
have been very courfely *ufed by the*
Tongues *and* pennes *of thefe men, yet*
fhall I never give your Majeftie *any*
fower counfell ; *I fhall rather magnifie*
your Clemencie, *that proceeded with*
thefe Offenders *in a* Court *of* Mercie
as well as Iuftice : *Since (as the* Reverend Iudges *then declared) you might*
have juftly called the Offendors *into*
another Court, *and put them to it in a*
way that might have exacted their
Lives, *for their ftirring (as much as in*
them lay) of mutinie *and* fedition.
Yet this I fhall be bold to fay, and
your Majefty *may confider of it in your*
Wifdom; That one way of Government

is not alwaies either fit or safe, *when the* Humors *of the* people *are in a continuall* Change. *Especially, when such men as these shall worke upon* your people, *and labour to infuse into them such malignant* Principles, *to introduce a* Parity *in the* Church *or* Common-wealth. Et, si non satis suâ sponte insaniant, instigare, *And to spur on such among them as are too sharply set already :* And *by this meanes make and prepare all advantages for the* Roman *party to scorne* Us, *and pervert them.*

I pray God blesse Your Majestie, Your Royall Consort, *and* Your hopefull Posterity, *That You may Live in* happinesse; *Govern with* Wisdom; *Support Your people by* Iustice; *Relieve them by* Mercy; *Defend them by* power
and

and fucceffe; *And Guide them in the* true Religion *by Your Lawes and moſt* Religious Example, *all the long and laſting dayes of Your* Life : *Which are and ſhall be the daily* prayers *of*

Your Sacred Majefties moft
loyall SUBIECT,

A N D,

Moft dutifull SERVANT,
as moft bound,

W. Cant.

MY LORDS,

 Shall not need to
fpeake of the infa-
mous courfe of *Li-
belling* in any kind :
Nor of the *punifh-
ment* of it, which in
fome cafes was *Capitall* by the *Imperi-
all Lawes*. As appeares*:
Nor how *patiently* fome great Men,
very great Men indeed, have borne
Animo civili (that's *Sueton* : his word*)
laceratam exiftimationem, The tearing
and rending of their credit and repu-

* *Cod. l. 9.*
T. 36.

* *Jn Iul.*
c. 75.

B   tation,

tation, with a gentle, nay, a generous minde.

But of al *Libels*, they are most *odious* which pretend *Religion:* As if that of all things did desire to bee defended by a *Mouth that is like an open Sepulcher,* or by a Pen that is made of a ficke and a loathfome Quill.

There were times when *Perfecutions* were great in the *Church,* even to exceed *Barbarity* it felfe : did any *Martyr* or *Confeffor,* in thofe times, *Libel* the *Governours?* Surely no; not one of them to my beft *remembrance:* yet thefe complaine of *Perfecution* without all fhew of caufe; and in the meane time *Libel* and rayle without all meafure. So little of kin are they to thofe which *fuffer for* Chrift, or the leaft part of *Chriftian Religion.*

My Lords, it is not every mans
fpirit

spirit to hold up againſt the *Venome* which *Libellers* ſpit. For S. *Ambroſe,* who was a ſtout and a worthy *Pre-late,* tels us, not that himſelfe, but that a far greater Man than he, that's K. *David,* had found out (ſo it ſeemes in his *judgment* 'twas no matter of ordi-nary ability) *Grande inventū,* a great and mighty invention, how to ſwal-low and put off thoſe bitter *Contume-lies* of the *tongue* *: and thoſe of the *pen* are no whit leſſe, and ſpread farther. And it was a great one indeed, and wel beſeemed the greatnes of *David.* But *I think* it wil be far better for me to look upward, and *practiſe* it, than to look downward, and *diſcourſe* upon it.

In the meane time I ſhal remember what an *Ancient* under the name of S. *Hierom* tels me *, *Indignū eſt & præpo-ſterū,* 'tis unworthy in it ſelfe, and pre-

*In Apol.*1. *David, c.*6.

Ad Ocean.de Ferend.Op-prob.

B 2   poſterous

posterous in demeanour for a man to bee ashamed for *doing good*, becaufe other men glory in *speaking ill*.

And I can fay it clearly and truly, as in the *presence of God*, I have done nothing, as a *Prelate*, to the uttermoft of what I am confcious, but with a *single heart*, and with a *fincere intention* for the good *Government* and *Honour* of the *Church*; and the maintenance of the *Orthodox Truth* and *Religion* of *Chriſt* profefled, eftablifhed, and maintained in this *Church* of *England*.

For my *care of this Church*, the reducing of it into *Order*, the upholding of the *Externall Worfhip of God* in it, and the fetling of it to the *Rules* of its *firſt Reformation*, are the *caufes* (and the fole caufes, what ever are pretended) of all this malicious *ſtorme*, which hath lowred fo black *upon Me*, & fome of

of *my Brethren.* And in the meane
time, they which are the only, or the
chief *Innovators* of the *Chriſtian world,*
having nothing to ſay, accuſe us of
Innovation; *They themſelves* and their
Complices in the meane time being the
greateſt *Innovators* that the *Chriſtian
world* hath almoſt ever known. I de-
ny not but others have ſpread more
dangerous *Errors* in the *Church* of
Chriſt; but no men, in any age of it,
have been more guilty of *Innovation*
than they, while themſelves cry out
againſt it : *Quis tulerit Gracchos ?*

And I ſaid wel, *Quis tulerit Gracchos?*
For 'tis moſt *apparent* to any man that
will not winke, that the *Intention* of
theſe men, and their *Abettors,* was and
is to raiſe a *Sedition,* being as great *In-
cendiaries* in the *State* (where they get
power) as they have ever been in the

Church; *Novatian* himſelfe hardly greater.

Burton Apo. p. 110.

Our maine *Crime* is (would they al ſpeak out, as ſome of them do) that we are *Biſhops*; were we not ſo, ſome of us might be as *paſſable* as other men. And a great trouble 'tis to them, that we maintain that our *calling of Biſhops* is *Iure Divino*, by Divine Right: Of this I have ſaid enough, and in this place, in *Leightons* Caſe, nor will I re-peate. Only this I will ſay, and abide by it, that the *Calling of Biſhops* is *Iure Divino*, by Divine Right, though not all *Adjunĉts* to their *calling*. And this I ſay in as direĉt *oppoſition* to the *Church of Rome*, as to the *Puritan humour*.

And I ſay farther, that from the *Apoſtles times*, in all ages, in all places, the *Church of Chriſt* was governed by *Biſhops*: And *Lay-Elders* never heard of, of, till *Calvins* new-fangled device at *Geneva.*

Now this is made by thefe men, as if it were *Contra Regem*, againſt the King, in right or in power.

But that's a meere *ignorant ſhift;* for our being *Biſhops, Jure divino,* by Divine Right, takes nothing from the *Kings Right or power over us.* For though our *Office* be from *God* and *Chriſt immediately*, yet may wee not *exerciſe* that *power*, either of *Order* or *Iuriſdiction*, but as *God* hath *appointed* us, that is, not in his *Majeſties*, or any *Chriſtian Kings Kingdomes*, but by and under the power of the *King* given us ſo to doe.

And were this a good *Argument* againſt us, as *Biſhops*, it muſt needs be good againſt *Prieſts* and *Mini-ſters* too ; for themſelves grant that their

their *Calling* is *Iure Divino*, by Divine Right; and yet I hope they will not fay,that to be *Prieſts and Miniſters* is againſt the *King*, or any His *Royall Prerogatives*.

Next,fuppofe our *Callings*, as *Biſhops*, could not bee made good *Iure Divino*,by Divine Right; yet *Iure Eccleſiaſtico*, by Eccleſiaſticall Right it cannot bee denyed. And here in *England* the *Biſhops* are confirmed, both in their power and meanes, by *Aƈt of Parliament*. So that here we ſtand in as good cafe, as the prefent *Lawes* of the *Realme* can make us. And fo we muſt ſtand,till the *Lawes* ſhall bee repealed by the fame *power* that made them.

Now then, *ſuppoſe* we had no other ſtring to hold by (I fay fuppofe this, but I grant it not) yet no man

can

can *Libell* againſt our *Calling* (as theſe men doe) bee it in *Pulpit, print,* or otherwiſe, but hee *Libels* againſt the *King* and the *State,* by whoſe *Lawes* wee are eſtabliſhed. Therefore, all theſe *Libels,* ſo farre forth as they are againſt our *Calling,* are againſt the *King* and the *Law,* and can have no other purpoſe, than to ſtirre up *ſedition* among the people.

If theſe men had any other *intention,* or if they had any Chriſtian or charitable deſire, to *reforme* any thing amiſſe; why did they not modeſtly *Petition His Majeſty* about it, that in his *Princely wiſedome* he might ſet all things right, in a *Juſt* and *Orderly* manner? But this was neither their *intention,* nor *way.* For one clamours out of his *Pulpit,* and all of them from the *Preſſe,* and in a moſt viru-

C   lent

lent and *unchriſtian* manner ſet themſelves to make a *heat* among the people; and ſo by *Mutiny*, to effect that,
which by *Law* they cannot; And,
by moſt falſe and unjuſt *Calumnies* to
defame both our *Callings* and *Per-*
ſons. But for *my part*, as I pitty their
rage, ſo I heartily pray *God* to *forgive*
their malice.

No *Nation* hath ever appeared
more jealous of *Religion*, then the
people of *England* have ever beene.
And their *zeale to Gods glory* hath
beene, and at this day is a great *ho-*
nour to them. But this *Zeale* of
theirs, hath not beene at all times
and in all perſons, alike guided by
knowledge. Now *Zeale*, as it is
of *excellent* uſe, where it ſees it's
way; ſo is it very *dangerous* com-
pany, where it goes on in the
darke:

darke : And thefe men, knowing the *Difpofition* of the people have laboured nothing more, than to mif-inform their *knowledge*, and mifguide their *Zeale*, and fo to fire that into a *fedition*, in hope that they, whom they cauflefly hate, might mifcarry in it.

For the *maine fcope* of thefe *Libels* is, to kindle a *Fealoufie* in mens mindes, that there are fome great plots in hand, *dangerous plots* (fo fayes Mr. *Burton* exprefly) to change the *Orthodox Religion* eftabli-fhed in *England*; and to bring in, *I* know not what, *Romifh fuperftition* in the roome of it. As if the *externall decent worfhip of* G o d could not bee upheld in this *Kingdome*, with-

C 2   out

a *You may fee it in the Example of S. Paul him-felfe, whofe very zeale in the darkneffe of his Un-derftanding, which hee then had, made him perfe-cute Chrift & his Church, Act. 22. 3, 4. And hee was very dangerous com-pany then; for he breath'd out threatnings againſt the Difciples, Act. 9. 1. So true is that of Saint Greg.Naz.Orat. 11. Ze-lus Iracundiam acuit: All zeale puts an edge to anger it felfe. And that muſt needs be dangerous in the darke.*

Page 5.

out bringing in of *Popery*.

Now by this *Art* of theirs, give me leave to tell you, that the *King* is moſt deſperately abuſed and wounded in the minds of his *people*; and the *Prelates* ſhamefully.

The King moſt deſperately: for there is not a more cunning tricke in the world, to *withdraw* the peoples hearts from their *Soveraign*, than to perſwade them that he is changing *true Religion*, and about to bring in groſſe *Superſtition* upon them.

And the Prelates ſhamefully; For they are charged to *ſeduce*, and lay the plot, and be the *Inſtruments*.

For his Majeſty firſt. This I know, and upon this *occaſion* take it my *duty* to ſpeak: There is no *Prince* in *Chriſtendome* more ſincere in his *Religion*, nor more conſtant to it, than the *King*.

King. And he gave fuch a Teftimony of this at his being in *Spain,* as I much doubt, whether the beft of that *Faction* durft have done halfe fo much, as his *Majefty* did, in the face of that *King- dome.* And this you my *Lord,* the *Earle* of *Holland,* and other Perfons of *ho- nour,* were eye and eare-witneffes of, having the happineffe to *attend* Him there. And at this day, as His. *Maiefty* (by *Gods* great blefsing both on him and us) *knowes* more, fo is he more *fet- led* and more confirmed, both in the *Truth* of the *Religion* here eftabli- fhed and in *Refolution* to maintaine it.

And for the Prelates; I affure my felfe, they cannot be fo bafe, as to live *Prelates* in the Church of *England,* & labour to bring in the *Superftitions* of the *Church of Rome,* upon themfelves and it. And if any fhould be fo *foule,* I

C 3   doe

do not only leave him to *Gods Judge-*
ment, but (if thefe *Libellers*, or any
other, can *difcover* that his bafe and
irreligious falfhood)to *fhame* alfo,and
fevere *punifhment* from the *State*: And
in any *juft* way, no mans *hand* fhal be
more,or fooner againft him,than *mine*
fhall be.

And for my felfe,to paffe by all the
fcandalous reproaches, which they
have moft *injurioufly* caft upon me, I
fhall fay this onely.

Firft, I know of no plot, nor *purpofe*
of *altering* the *Religion* eftablifhed.

Secondly, I have ever beene farre
from attempting any thing that may
truly be faid to *tend* that way in the
leaft degree : and to thefe two I here
offer my *Oath*.

Thirdly, if the *King* had a mind to
change *Religion*, (which I know hee
hath

hath not, and GOD forbid hee should
ever have) he must seek for other *In-
struments*. For as basely as these men
conceive of me, yet I thanke GOD, I
know my duty well both to GOD and
the *King*: And I know that al the *duty*
I owe to the *King*, is under GOD. And
my great happinesse it is (though not
mine alone, but your *Lordships* and all
his subiects with me) that we live under a *Gracious* and a *Religious King*,
that will ever give us leave to serve
GOD first, and *Him next*. But were
the daies otherwise, I thank *Christ* for
it, I yet *know* not how to serve any
man against the *Truth* of GOD, and I
hope I shall never learne it.

But to returne to the businesse: what
is their *Art* to make the world believe
a *change* of *Religion* is endevoured?
What? vvhy, *forsooth*, they say,
there

there are great *Innovations* brought
in by the *Prelates,* and such as tend
to the advancing of *Popery.*

Now that the *Vanity* and *falshood* of
this may appear, I shall humbly desire
your *Lordships* to give me leave to re-
cite briefly al the *Innovations* charged
upon us, be they of lesse or greater *moment,* and as briefly to answer them.
And then you shall clearely see, whether any *cause* hath bin given of these
unsavoury *Libels*; and withall, whether there bee any shew of *cause* to
feare a *change of Religion.* And I will
take these great pretended *Innovations* in order, as I meet with them.

First, I begin with the *Newes
from Ipswich.*

Pag. 2. Where the *first *Innovation is, that
the last yeeres Fast was enjoyned to bee
without*

without Sermons in London , *the Sub-*
urbs , and other infected places , contrary
to the Orders for other Fasts in former
times : Whereas Sermons are the onely
meanes to humble men, &c.

To this I fay *First,* That an after-
age may, without *offence,* learn to avoid
any vifible *Inconvenience* obferved in
the former. And there was vifible *In-*
convenience obferved in mens former
flocking to *Sermons* in *Infected places.*
Secondly, This was no particular
Act of the *Prelates* ; but the bufineffe
was debated at the *Councell-Table,* being a matter of *State,* as well as of *Reli-*
gion. And it was concluded for no *Ser-*
mons in those infected places, upon this
Reafon; That *infected Perfons* or *Fami-*
lies, knowne in their owne *Parifhes,*
might not take occafion upon thofe
D   *by-dayes*

by-dayes to runne to other *Churches*, where they were not knowne, as many ufe to doe, to heare fome *humorous* men preach; For on the *Sundayes*, when they better kept their owne *Churches:* the *danger* is not fo great altogether.

Nor *Thirdly* is that true, that *Sermons* are the *Onely meanes* to *humble* men. For though the *preaching* of *Gods word*, where it is performed according to his *Ordinance*, be a great meanes of many good *effects* in the *foules* of Men; Yet no *Sermons* are the only *meanes* to *humble* Men. And fome of their *Sermons* are fitter a great deale for other *operations* : Namely, to ftir up *fedition*, as you may fee by Mr. *Burtons*; for this his printed *Libel* was a *Sermon* firft, & a *Libell* too. And 'tis the beft part of a *Faft* to abftaine from fuch *Sermons*.

2. *The second Innovation is.* *That *Wednesday was appointed for the Fast-day, and that this was done with this intention, by the example of this Fast without preaching, to suppresse all the Wednesday-Lectures* in London. *Pag. 3.

To this I anſwer *First,* that the appointing of *Wednesday* for the *Fast-day* was no *Innovation.* For it was the *day* in the *last Faſt* before this : and *I my* *elfe* remember it ſo, above forty yeares ſince, more than once.

Secondly, if there had beene any *Innovation* in it, the *Prelates* named not the *day*; my *Lord Keeper,* I muſt *appeale* to your *Lordſhip* : The *day* was firſt named by your *Lordſhip,* as the *uſuall,* and *fitteſt* day. And yet I dare *ſay,* and *ſweare too,* that your *Lordſhip* had no aime to bring in *Popery* ; nor to ſuppreſſe al, or any the *Wednesday-Lectures*

D 2   in

in *London.* *Befides*, thefe men live to fee the *Faſt* ended, and no one *Wednefday Lecture* fuppreffed.

Pag. 3. 3. *The third Innovation* is, that the Prayer for feafonable weather was pur- ged out of this laſt Faſt-booke, which was* (fay they) *one caufe of Ship-wracks and tempeſtuous weather.*

To this I fay, *Firſt* in the *Generall;* This *Faſt-bcoke*, and all that have formerly beene made, have beene both made, aud publifhed by the command of the *King*, in whofe fole power it is *to call a Faſt.* And the *Arch B.* and *Biſhops* to whom the or- dering of the *book* is committed, have *power* under the *King*, to *put in*, or *leave out*, whatfoever they thinke fit for the prefent *occafion;* As their *Pre- deceffors* have ever done before them.

Provided

Provided that nothing be in contrary to the *Doctrine* or *Discipline* of the *Church of England*.

And this may serve in the *Generall* for all *Alterations*, in that or any other *Fast-booke* or bookes of Devotion upon any particular occasions, which may and ought to *vary* with severall *times*, and we may, and doe, and will *justifie*, under *His Maiesties power* all such *Alterations* made therein.

Secondly, for the *particular*. *When* this *last booke* was set out, the weather was very *seasonable*. And it is not the *custome* of the *Church*, nor *fit* in it *selfe* to pray for *seasonable* weather when we *have* it, but when we *want* it. When the *former booke* was set out, the weather was *extreame ill*, and the Harvest in *danger* ; Now

D 3   the

the Harveſt was in, and the weather good.

Thirdly, 'tis moſt *inconſequent* to ſay, that the leaving that Prayer out of the *booke* of *devotions*, cauſed the *Ship-wrackes* and the *Tempeſts*, which fol-lowed. And as bold they are with *God Almighty*, in ſaying it was the *cauſe :* For ſure I am, God never told them, that was the cauſe. And if *G O D* never *revealed* it, they cannot come to know it ; yet had the *Bi-ſhops* beene *Prophets*, and foreſeene theſe *Accidents*, they would certainly have *prayed* againſt them.

Fourthly, Had any *Miniſter* found it *neceſſary* to uſe this *prayer* at any one time during the Faſt, he might with eaſe, and without danger, have ſup-plied that want, by uſing that *prayer* to the ſame purpoſe which is in the Ordinary *Liturgy*.   *Fifthly,*

Fiftbly, I humbly defire your *Lordſhips* to weigh well the *Conſequence* of
this great, and dangerous *Innovation.*
The Prayer for faire *weather* was left
out of the *Book* for the *Faſt*; Therfore
the *Prelates* intend to bring in *Popery.*
An excellent *Conſeqnence*, were there
any ſhew of Reaſon in it.

4. *The Fourth Innovation* * *is, That* **Pag.3.*
*there is one very uſefull Colleɛt left out, and
a Clauſe omitted in another.*

To this I anſwer *Firſt*, As before; It
was *lawfull* for us to *alter* what we
thought fit.

And *Secondly*, ſince that *Colleɛt* made
mention of *Preaching*, and the *Aɛt* of
State forbad *Sermons* on the *Faſt dayes
in infeɛted places*; we thought it fit, in
purſuance of that *Order*, to leave out
that *Colleɛt.*

And

And *Thirdly*, for the branch in the
other, wch is the *first Collect*, Though
God did deliver our *forefathers* out of
Romish superstition, yet (*God* be *blessed*
for it) we were never *in*. And therefore · that *clause* being *unfittingly* ex-
pressed, we thought fit to passe it over.

'Pag. 3. 5 *The fitfh Innovation* * *is*, *That in
the sixth Order for the Fast, there is a paf-
sage left out concerning the abuse of Fasting in relation to merit.*

To this I *answer*. That he to whom
the *ordering* of that *Booke* to the *Presse*
was *committed*, did therefore *leave* it
out; Becaufe in this *Age* and *Kingdome*
there is little opinion of *meriting by
Fasting*.
Nay, on the contrary, the contempt
and fcorne of all *fasting* (fave what
humorous men call for of themfelves) is
fo

fo ranke, that it would grieve any *Chriſtian* man to fee the neceſſary *Orders of the Church concerning Faſting*, both in *Lent*, and at other *ſet times*, ſo *vilified* as they are.

6. *The Sixth Innovation* * *is, That* * Pag. 2. *the Lady Elizabeth and her Princely Children are daſhed* (that's their phraſe) *out of the new Collect, whereas they were in the Collect of the former Booke.*

For this *Firſt*, The *Author* of the *Newes* knowes full well that they are left out of the *Collect* in the latter *Editions* of the *Common Praier-Book*, aſwel as in the *Booke* for the *Faſt*. And this was done according to the *Courſe* of the *Church*, which *ordinarily names* none in the Praier, *but the Right line deſcending*. Yet this was not done till the *King* himſelf *commanded* it; As I have

E   to

to shew under *his* *Majesties* hand.

Secondly, I beseech your *Lordships* to consider, what must be the *Consequence* here: The *Queene* of *Bohemia* and her *Children* are left out of the *Collect*, therfore the *Prelates* intend to bring in *Popery*; For *that* (you know) they say is the end of all these *Innovations*. Now if this be the end and the *Consequence*; Truly the *Libellers* have done very dutifully to the *King*, to *poyson* his *people* with this conceit; That the *Lady* *Elizabeth* and her *Children* would keepe *Popery* out of this *Kingdom*, but the *King* and his *Children* will not. And many as good *offices* as these have they done the *King* quite thorow these *Libels*, and quite thorow his *Kingdoms*. For *My part*, I *honour* the *Queene* of *Bohemia*, and her *Line*, as much as any man whatsoever, and shall be as ready

to

to *ſerve* them, but I know not how to
depart from my *Allegeance*, as I doubt
theſe men have done.

7. *The Seventh Innovation* * *is, That* * Pag. 8.
*theſe words (who art the Father of thine
Elect and of their ſeed) are changed in
the Preface of that Collect, which is for
the Prince, and the Kings Children.*
And, with a moſt ſpitefull inference,
That *this was done by the Prelates to ex-
clude the Kings Children out of the number of Gods Elect.* And they call it *an
intollerable impietie and horrid treaſon.*

To this I *anſwer, Firſt,* That this
Alteration was made in my *Predeceſ-
ſors* time before I had any *Authority* to
meddle with theſe things, further then
I was *called* upon by him.

Secondly, This is not therefore to lay
any aſperſion upon my *Predeceſſor,* for

E 2   he

he did in that but his dutie : For his *Majestie* acknowledges, it was done by his *speciall direction*, as having then no *Children* to *pray* for.

And *Thirdly*, this *Collect* could not be very *old*, for it had no being in the *Common Prayer Book* all Q. *Elizabeths* time, she having no *Issue*.

The truth is, it was made at the comming in of K. I A M E S; and must of necessitie be *changed* over and over againe *pro ratione Temporum*, as *Times* and Persons varie. And this is the *Intolerable Impiety*, *and horrid Treason* they *charge* upon *Us*.

In this *Method* the *Innovations* are set down in the *Newes from Ipswich*. But then in Mr. *Burtons Newes from Friday-street* (called his *Apologie*) they are in an other Order, and more are added. Therefore with your *Lord-*

ships

ſhips leave I will not *repeat* any of theſe, but goe on to the *reſt*, which Mr. *Burton* addes.

8. *The eighth Innovation* ✶ *is , That* ✶ *Burtons Apologie,* *in the Epiſtle the Sunday before Eaſter,* *pag. 2.* *we have put out* In *, and made it ,* At the Name *of* Ieſus *every knee ſhall bow*; *which alteration ,* he ſaith , *is directly againſt the Act of Parliament.*

Here give mee leave to tell you 'tis *At the* Name *of* Jeſus, in the late learned *Tranſlation* made in K. IAMES his time. About which many learned Men of beſt note in the *Kingdom* were imployed, beſides ſome *Prelates.*

But to this I anſwer: Firſt, 'Tis true, the *Common Prayer Book* was *confirmed* by *Act of Parliament,* and ſo all things contained in it, at the paſsing of that *Act.* But I hope if any thing were

E 3   falſe

falſe *printed* then, the *Parliament* did
not intend to paſſe thoſe ſlips for cur-
rent.

Secondly, I am not of opinion, that if
one *word* be put in for another, ſo they
beare both the ſame *ſenſe*, that there
is any great matter done againſt the
Act of Parliament.

Thirdly, this can make no *Innovati-
on.* For In *the Name*, and At *the
Name of* Ieſus, can make no *Eſſentiall
difference* here And Mr. *Pryn* (whoſe
Darling buſineſſe it hath long been to
cry downe the *honour* due to the *Son* of
God, at the *mentioning* of his *ſaving
Name* IESVS) knowes the *Grammar
Rule* well, *In a place, or at a place,* &c.

Fourthly, if there were any error in
the change of *In* into *At*; I do here *ſo-
lemnly proteſt* to you, I know not how
It came: For *authority* from the *Pre-*
lates

lates,the *Printers* had none,and fuch a word is eafily changed in fuch a *negli-gent Preſſe* as we have in *England*. Or if any *altered* it purpofely, for ought I know, they did it to *gratifie* the *Preci-fer* fort. For therin they followed the *Geneva Tranſlation*, & printed at *Ge-neva*, 1557 *. where the words are, *At the Name of* I E S V S. And that is ninety foure yeares agoe; and there-fore no *Innovation* made by us.

* *In O-ctavo.*

    Fiftly,this I find in the *Queenes In-junctions* *, without either word, *In* or *At. When ſoever the Name of Jeſus ſhal be in any leſſon,Sermon, or otherwiſe pronounced in the Church('tis injoined) that due reverence be made of al perſons, young and old, with lowlineſſe of Courſy, and uncovering of the heads of the men-kind, as therunto doth neceſſarily belong, and heretofore hath beene accuſtomed.*

* *Injuncti-on 52.*

                              So

So here's *neceßitie* laid upon it, and *cuftome* for it, and both expreſſed by *Authoritie* in the very *beginning* of the *Reformation*; and is therefore no *Innovation now.*

* Pag. 3. 9. *The Ninth Innovation* * *is, That two places are changed in the Praiers fet forth for the fifth of November: And ordered to be read* (they ſay) *by Act of Parliament. The firſt place is changed thus, From, Root out that Babyloniſh and Antichriſtian Sect, which ſay of Jeruſalem,* &c. *Into this forme of words. Root out that Babyloniſh & Antichriſtian Sect* (*of them*)*which ſay,* &c. The ſecond place went thus in the old : *Cut off theſe workers of iniquity, whoſe Religion is Rebellion.* But in the booke printed 1635. 'tis thus altered : *Cut off thoſe workers of Iniquity, who turne Religion into Rebellion,* &c.   To

To this I fay *Firft*, 'Tis a *notorious untruth*, that this *Booke* was *ordered* to be *read* by *Act of Parliament*. The *Act of Parliament* indeed is *printed* before it; and therein is a *Command* for *Prayers* and *Thankefgivings* every *fifth of November*: but not one word or fyllable for the *Forme of Prayer*. That's left to the *Church*, therefore here's no *Innovation* againft that *Act of Parliament*.

Secondly, The *Alteration* firft mentioned, that is, *That Sect*, or *That Sect of them*: is of fo fmall *confequence*, as 'tis not worth the fpeaking of. Befides if there be any thing of *moment* in it, 'tis anfwered in the next.

Thirdly, both for *that* and the *fecond place*, which feemes of more *moment*; & fo for the reft not only in that *Book*, but that other alfo for his *Majefties Coronation*; *His Majeftie* exprefly com-

F   manded

manded *Me* to make the *Alterations*, and fee them *printed.* And here are both the *Bookes* with his *Majesties warrant* to each of them. So that here-in I conceive I did not *offend*, unlesse it were that I gave not thefe men *notice* of it, or asked them leave to obey the K I N G.

Againft this there can be but two *objections*, fhould *malice* it felfe goe to work. *The one is, that I moved his Majefty to command the Change. And the other, that now, when I faw my felfe challeng d for it, I procured His Majefties hand for my fecurity.*

To thefe *I anfwer* cleerly; *Firft,* that I did not move the *King, directly,* or *indirectly;* to make this *change.*

And *Secondly,* that I had His Majefties hand to the *Booke,* not *now,* but *then,* and before ever I caufed them to be

(35)

be *printed*, as now they are. And th3t both thefe are *true*, I here againe *freely* offer my felfe to my *Oath*.

And yet *Fourthly*, that you may fee *His gracious Majeftie* uf:d not his *power* only in *comm1nding* this *change* ; but his *wifdome* alfo ; I fhall adventure to give you my *Reafons*, fuch as they are, why this *Alteration* was moft *fit*, if not *neceffary*.

My *firft Reafon is*, In the *Lita-* ny in *Hen*. 8. his time [a] : and alfo under *Edw*. 6. [b] there was this *Claufe: From the tyrany of the Bi-fhop of Rome, and all his deteftable enormities, frõ al falf doctrine, &c. Good Lord deliver us.* But in the *Litany* in Q. *Elizabeths* time this *Claufe* about the *Pope* was left out, and it feemes of *purpofe*, for avoiding of *fcandall* : And yet the *Prelates* for

[a] *It was put into the Litany of H. 8 his time, as appeares in his Primer, with his Injunction before it.*

[b] *And 'tis in both the Service Bookes of Ed. 6. both that which was printed, 1549. And in that which was after, Ann. 1552,*

F 2   that

that not accounted *Innovators*, or *Jn-troducers* of *Popery*. Now 'tis a farre greater *scandall* to call their *Religion* Rebellion, then 'tis to call their chiefe *Bishop Tyrant*.

And this R*eason* is drawne from *scandall*, which muſt ever be avoided as much as it may.

My *second* Reaſon is, that the *learned* make but *three* R*eligions* to have been of old in the world, *Paganiſme*, *Iudaiſme*, and *Chriſtianitye*. And now they have added a *fourth*, which is *Turciſme*, and is an abſurd *mixture* of the other three. Now if this *ground* of theirs be true (as 'tis *generally* received) peihaps it will be of *dangerous* conſequence ſadly to *avow*, that the *Popiſh* Religion is Rebellion. That ſome *opinions* of theirs teach *rebellion*, *on*, that's *apparently* true, the *other* would be *thought on*, to fay no more. And this *Reafon* well weighed , is taken from the very *foundations* of *Religion* it felfe.

My *Third Reafon* is, Becaufe if you make their *Religion* to be *Rebellion*, then you make their Religion., and Rebellion to be all *one*. And that is againft the *ground* both of *State*, and the *Law*. For when diverfe *Romifh Priefts* and *Iefuites* have defervedly fuffered *death* for *Treafon*, is it not the conftant and juft profefsion of the *State*, that they never put any man to *death* for Religion, but for Rebellion and *Treafon* onely? Doth not the *State* truly *affirme*, that there was never any *Law* made againft the *life* of a *Papift*, *quatenus* a *Papift* onely? And

F 3   is

is not all this ſtarke *falſe* , if their very *Religion* be Rebellion ? For if their Religion be Rebellion , it is not onely *falſe* , but *impoſſible* , that the *ſame man* in the *ſame Act* ſhould ſuffer for his *Rebellion* , and not for his *Religion*.

And this *King James* of ever *bleſſed memory* underſtood paſſing well, when (in his *premonition* to all *Chriſti-* an *Monarches* *) he ſaith , *J doe conſtantly maintaine that no Papiſt either in my time, or in the time of the late Queen, ever dyed for his conſcience.* Therfore he did not thinke , their very *Religion* was *Rebellion.* Though this *Clauſe* paſſed through *In advertencie* in his time. And this *Reaſon* is grounded both upon the *practiſe* , and the *Iuſtice* of the *Law.*

Which of theſe *Reaſons* , or whether

* Pag. 336.

ther any other better, were in His *Majesties* thoughts, when he commanded the *Alteration* of this *clause*, I know not. But I tooke it my *duty* to lay it before you, that the *King* had not onely *power*, but *Reason* to command it.

10. The *Tenth Innovation* * *is,* *That* * *Pag. 3.* the *Prayer for the Navy is left out of the late booke for the Fast.*

To this I *say*, there is great *Reason* it should. For the *King* had no declared *Enemy* then, nor (*God* be thanked) hath he *now*. Nor had he *then* any *Navy* at Sea. For almost all the *Ships* were come *in*, before the *Fastbooke* was set out.

But howsoever, an excellent *consequence* it is, if you mark it; The *prayer* for the *Navy* was left *out* of the

Booke

booke for the *Faſt*, therefore by that, and ſuch like *Innovations* the *Pre-lates* intend to bring *in Popery*. Indeed, if that were a piece of the *Pre-lates* plots to bring in *Popery* from beyond Sea, then they were mightily overſeene that they left out the *prayer* for the *Navy*. But elſe what *reaſon* or *conſequence* is in it, I know not, unleſſe perhaps **Mr.** *Burton* intended to befriend **Dr.** *Baſtwicke*, and in the *Navy* bring hither the *Whore of Babylon* to be ready for his *Chriſtening*, as hee moſt prophanely ſcoffes.

Well: I pray G o d the time come not upon this *Kingdome*, in which it will be found, that no one thing hath *advanced* or *Uſherd* in *Po-pery* ſo faſt, as the *groſſe Abſurdities* even in the *Worſhip of God*, which
theſe

thefe *Men*, and their *like,maintaine*
both in *Opinion* and *practife*.

11. *The eleventh Innovation, is the* * Page 105
reading of the fecond Service at the
Communion-Table, or the Altar.

To this *firft* I can truly fay, that
fince my owne *memory*, this was in
ufe in very many places, as being
moft *proper* (for thofe *prayers* are
then read which both precede and
follow the *Communion*,) and by little and little this *Auncient cuftome*
was *altered*, and in thofe places firft,
where the *Emiffaries* of this *faction*
came to *preach*. And now if any
in *Authority* offer to *reduce* it, this
auncient courfe of the *Church* is by
and by called an *Innovation*.

Secondly, with this the *Rubricks*
of the *Common-prayer booke* agree:
G   for

for the *firſt Rubricke* after the *Com-munion* tels us, that upon *Holy-dayes*, though there be no *Communion*, yet *all* els that's appointed at the Com-munion ſhall be read. *Shall be read?* That's true, but where? Why, the laſt *Rubricke* before the *Commu-nion* tels us, that the Prieſt, ſtanding at the *North ſide* of the *Holy Table*, *ſhall ſay the Lords Prayer, with that which followes.* So that not only the *Communion*, but the *prayers* wch ac-company the *Communion* (which are commonly call'd the *Second ſervice*) are to bee read at the *Communion-Table*. Therefore if this be an *In-novation*, tis made by the *Rubricke*, not by the *Prelates* ; And Maſter Burtons ſcoffe that this *ſecond ſer-vice muſt be ſerved in for dainties* *, ſa-vours too much of *Belly* and *pro-phanation.* 12 One

* *Pag.* 105.
[*Then the Second ſer-vice, as dain-ties, muſt bee ſaid there.*]

12 One thing ſtickes much in their ſtomacks, and they call it an *Innovation** too. And that is, *bow-* *Pag.105.* *ing, or doing Reverence at our firſt comming into the Church, or at our nearer approaches to the Holy Table, or the Altar*, (call it whether you will) In which they will needs have it, *that we worſhip the Holy Table, or God knowes what.*

To this I *anſwer*. *Firſt*, That *God* forbid we ſhould *worſhip* any thing but G o d Himſelfe.

Secondly, that if to *Worſhip* G o d when we *enter* into *his houſe*, or *approach* his *Altar*, bee an *Innovation*, tis a very *Old one.*

For *Moſes* did *reverence* at the very *doore* of the *Tabernacle*, *Num.* 20. *Hezekiah*, and all that *Num. 20.6*

G 2   were

were prefent with him, when they had made an *end of offering, howed and worſhipped,* (^d *2 Chron.* 29.) *David* cals the people to it with a *Venite, O come let us worſhip, and fall downe, and kneele before the Lord our Maker,* (^e *Pſal.*95.) And in *all* theſe places (I pray mark it) 'tis *bodily worſhip.*

d 2 Chron. 29.29.

e Pſal. 95,6.

Nor can they ſay, that this was *Judaicall* worſhip, and now not to be *imitated.* For long before *Judaiſme* began, *Bethel,* the *Houſe of* God, was a place of *Reverence,* (^f *Gen.* 28.) Therefore certainly, Of, and To God.

f Gen.28.17. &c.

And after *Judaicall worſhip* ended, *Venite, Adoremus,* as farre upwards as there is any track of a *Liturgie,* was the *Introitus* of the *Prieſt,* all the *Latine Church* over.

And in the daily *prayers* of the

Church

Church of *England;* this was *retained*
at the *Reformation;* and that *Pfalme,*
in which is *Venite, Adoremus;*is commanded to begin the *Morning Service* every Day. And for ought I
know, the *Prieſt* may as well leave
out the *Venite,* as the *Adoremus;*the
calling the people to their duty, as
the *duty* it ſelfe, when they are come.

Therefore even according to the
Service-booke of the *Church* of *England,* the *Prieſt* and the *People* both
are called upon, for *externall* and *bodily Reverence* and *Worſhip* of G o d
in his *Church.* Therefore they which
do it, doe not *Innovate.* And yet the
Government is ſo *moderate* (God grant
it be not too *looſe* therewhile) that
no man is *conſtrained,* no man *queſtio-
ned,* only *religiouſly* called upon, *Venite, Adoremus, Come, let us worſhip.*

For my owne part I take my felfe *bound* to *worſhip* with *Body*, as wel as in *Soule*, when ever I come where GOD is *worſhipped*. And were this *Kingdome* fuch as would allow no *Holy Table*, ſtanding in its proper place (and fuch *places* fome there are) yet I would *worſhip God* when I came into *His houſe*. And were the *times* fuch, as fhould beat downe *Churches*, and all the *curious carved worke thereof*, *with Axes, and Ham-* Pfal. 74 6. *mers*, as in *Pſal.*74. (and fuch *times* have beene)yet would *I worſhip* in what place foever I came to *pray*, though there were not fo much as a ſtone laid for *Bethel*. But this is the *miſery*; tis *ſuperſtition* now adaies for any man to come with more *Reve-rence* into a *Church*, then a *Tinker* & his *Butch* come into an *Ale-houſe*; the *Compariſon*

Comparison is too *homely*,but my *Juſt indignation* at the *profaneneſſe* of the times, makes me ſpeake it.

And you my *Honourable Lords* of the *Garter*,in your great *Solemnities*,you doe your *Reverence*,and to *Almighty God*,I doubt not,but yet it is *Verſus Altare*, towards his *Altar*, as the greateſt *place* of Gods *Reſidence* upon earth. (I *ſay* the *greateſt*, yea greater then the *Pulpit*. For *there* 'tis *Hoc eſt Corpus meum*, This is my Body. But in the *Pulpit*, tis at moſt, but ; *Hoc eſt Verbum meum*, This is my Word. And a *greater Reverence* (no doubt) is *due* to the *Body*, then to the *Word* of our *Lord*. And ſo,in *Relation*,*anſwerably* to the *Throne*,where his *Body* is uſually *preſent*; then to the *Seate*, whence His *Word* uſeth to be *Proclaimed*. And

God

God hold it *there*, at *His Word*; for, as
too many men ufe the matter, *'Tis
Hoc eft verbum Diaboli.. This is the
word of the Divell, in too *many* places. Witneffe Sedition, and the like
to it.) And this *Reverence* yee doe
when ye enter the *Chappel*, and when
you *approach* nearer to *offer*.　And
this is no *Innovation* , for you are
bound to it by your *Order*, and thats
not *New*,

　　And *Idolatry* it is not, to *worſhip* God towards His *Holy Table*;
For if it had beene *Idolatry*, I pre-
ſume *Queene Elizabeth* , *and King
Iames* would not have *practiſed* it,
no not in thoſe *Solemnities*.　And
being not *Idolatry* , but true *Divine
Worſhip*, *You* will, I hope, give a poor
Prieſt leave to *Worſhip* God, as *Your
ſelves* doe. For if it be *Gods Worſhip*,

　　　　　　　　　　　　　　　I

I *ought* to doe it as well as *You* : And
if it be *Idolatry, You ought not* to doe
it more than I.

I *say againe,* I hope a poore *Priest*
may *Worship God* with as lowly *Reverence* as you doe, since you are
bound by your *Order,* and by your
Oath, according to a *Constitution* of
Hen. the fifth, (as appeares [a]) to give [a] *In Libro.*
due *honour and Reverence, Domino* *Nigro.*
Deo, & Altari ejus, in modum viro- *Windesori-*
rum Ecclesiasticorum ; That is, to the *ensi. p. 65.*
Lord your God, and to His *Altar* (for
there is a *Reverence* due to that too,
though such as comes farre short of
Divine Worship) and this in the
Manner, as *Ecclesiasticall Persons*
both *Worship* and doe *Reverence.*

The *Story* which led in this *Decree* is this: *King Henry the fifth,* that
Noble and victorious Prince, return-

H   ing

ing *glorioufly* out of *France*, fat at this
Solemnitie; and finding the *Knights*
of the Order fcarce bow to *God*, or but
flightly, and then bow towards *Him*
and *His Seat*, *ftarted* at it (being a
Prince then grown as *religious*, as he
was before *victorious*,) and after ask-
ing the *reafon*; for til *then* the *Knights*
of the *Order* never *bowed* toward the
King or his *Seat*; the *Duke of Bed-*
ford anfwered, it was *fetled* by a *Chap-*
ter Act three yeares before.   Hereupon , that Great K I N G replied,
No, Ile none of this, till you the Knights
doe it Satis benè, *well enough, and with*
due performance to Almighty G O D.
And hereupon the forenamed *Act*
proceeded, that they fhould doe *this*
duty to Almighty God, not *flightly*,
but *Ad modum virorum Ecclefiaftico-*
rum, as *low, as well*, as *decently, as Cler-*
gie-men ufe to doe it.   *Now*

$\mathcal{N}$ ow if you will turne this off, and
fay, it was the *fuperftition* of that *Age*
fo to do ; Bifhop *Jewell* will come in
to *help Me* there. For where *Har-
ding* names divers *Ceremonies*, and
particularly bowing themfelves, and
adoring at the *Sacrament*, I fay, *adoring at* the *Sacrament*, not *adoring* the
Sacrament; there Bifhop *Jewel* (that
learned, painefull, and *reverend Pre-
late*) *approves all* both the *Kneeling*
and the *bowing*, and the *ftanding up*
at the *Gofpell* (which as *ancient* as it
is in the *Church*, and a common *cuftome*, is yet *fondly* made another of
their *Innovations*: [a]) And further, the
Bifhop addes *, *That they are all com-*
mendable geftures, and tokens of devo-
tion, fo long as the people underftand
what they meane, and apply them unto
G o d. Now with us the *people* did

[a] *B. Jewels
reply to
Hardings
anfwer. Art.
3. Div. 29.*

ever *understand* them *fully*,and *apply* them to God, and to none but *God*, till these *factious* spirits,and their *like*, to the great *dif-service* of *God* and his *Church*, went about to perswade them,that they are *superstitious*,if not *Idolatrous* gestures: As they make *every thing* else to be, where *God* is not served *slovenly*.

* Pag. 4. 5. 105. 13 *The Thirteenth Innovation* is: *The placing of the holy Table Altar-wise, at the upper end of the Chancell, that is, the setting of it North and South, and placing a Raile before it,* to keepe it from prophanation, *which* Mr. *Burton* sayes, *is done to advance and Usher in Popery.*

To this *I answer*, That 'tis no *Popery*,to set a *Raile* to keep *prophanation* from that *Holy Table* : nor is it any

any *Innovation* to *place* it at the *upper
end* of the *Chancell* as the *Altar* ftood.
And this appeares both by the *Practice*, and by the *Command* and
Canon of the *Church of England.*

   Firſt, by the *Practice* of the *Church
of England.* For in the *Kings Royall
Chappels*, and *divers Cathedrals*, the
Holy Table hath ever fince the *Reformation* ftood at the *upper end* of
the *Quire*, with the *large* or *full ſide*
towards the people.

   And though it ftood in moſt *Pariſh Churche* the *other way*, yet whether there be not more reaſon, the
Pariſh Churches fhould be made *con-
formable* to the *Cathedrall* and *Mo-
ther Churches*, than the *Cathedrals*
to them, I leave to any *reaſonable*
man to *judge.*

   And yet here is nothing done either

ther by *violence* or *command* to take
off the *Indifferency* of the standing
of the *Holy Table* either way, but
only by *laying* it *fairely* before men,
how fit it is there should bee *order*,
and *uniformity*; I say still reserving
the *Indifferency* of the standing.

But howsoever I would faine
know, how any *discreet moderate*
man dares say, that the placing of
the *Holy Table Altar-wise* (since they
will needs call it so) is done either
to advance or Usher in Popery? For
did *Queen Elizabeth* banish *Popery*,
and yet did she all along her *Raigne*
from *first* to *last* leave the *Communion Table so* standing in her owne
Chappell Royall, in Saint *Pauls* and
Westminster, and *other* places; and *all*
this of *purpose to advance* or *Usher in*
that *Popery* which shee had driven
out.   And

And since *her death* have two *Gracious Kings* kept out *Popery* all their *times*, and yet left the *Holy Table* standing, *as it did* in the *Queenes time*, and all of *purpose* to *advance* or *Usher in Popery* which they *kept out*?

Or what's the matter? May the *Holy Table* stand this way in the *Kings Chappell* or *Cathedrals*, or *Bishops Chappels*, and not elsewhere? *Surely*, if it be decent and *fit* for *Gods service*, it may stand *so* (if *Authority* please) in *any Church*. But if it *advance or Usher in any superstition* and *Popery*, it ought to *stand so* in *none*.

Nor hath any *Kings Chappell* any *Prerogative* (if *that* may bee called *one*) above any *ordinary Church* to *disserve God* in by any *Superstitious Rites*.

Rites. Where, give mee leave to tell you, that the *King* and his *Chappell* are moſt *jeeringly,* and with *ſcorne abuſed,* in the laſt leaſe of Mr. *Burtons Mutinous Appeale,* for ſuch it is.

Secondly, this appeares by the *Canon* or *Rule* of the *Church* of *England* too, for 'tis plaine in the laſt *Injunction* of the *Queene;* That the *Holy Table ought* to ſtand at the *upper end* of the *Quire, North and South,* or *Altar-wiſe.* For the words of the *Queenes Injunctions* are theſe.

The *Holy Table in every Church* (marke it I pray, not in the *Royall Chappel* or *Cathedrals only,* but in *every Church*) *ſhall be decently made and ſet in the place where the Altar ſtood.* Now the *Altar* ſtood at the *upper end* of the *Quire North* and *South,* as

appeares

appeares before by the *practise* of the Church. And there to set it otherwise, is to set it *crosse* the place, *not In* the place where the *Altar* stood : and so *Stulti dum vitant vitia--* weake men, as these *Libellers* are, run into one *Superstition,* while they would avoyd another ; For they runne upon the *superstition* of the *Crosse,* while they seeke to avoyd the *superstition* of the *Altar.* So you see here's neither *popery* nor *Innovation* in all the *practise* of *Queene Elizabeth,* or since.

These words of the *Injunction* are so *plaine,* as that they can admit of no shift.

And give me leave to tell you, that a very learned *Prelate* of this *Church,* and *one,* whom *I think* these men will not *accuse,* as a man like to

I   *advance*

advance or Usher in Popery, is of the same *opinion* : 'Tis my *Lord* the *Bishop* of *Salisbury*.

Some difference was lately rising about placing the *Communion-Table in a Parish Church* of his *Dioceße*. The *Bishop* carefull to prevent all *diforder*, fends his *Injunction* on under his *hand* and *feale* to the *Curate* and *Church-Wardens*, to *settle* that *bufineße*: In which hee hath thefe *two* paffages *remarkeable*. I have *feene* and *read* the *Order*.

The *firft paßage* is this; *By the Injunction of Queene Elizabeth* (faith hee) *and by Can. 82. under King James, the Communion Tables fhould ordinarily be fet and ftand with the fide to the Eaft wall of the Chancell.* Therfore this is no *Innovation*, fince there is *Injunction* and *Canon* for it.

May 17. 1637.

The

The *other* paſſage is this; *'Tis Ig-nornance* (ſaith that *learned Biſhop*) *to thinke that the ſtanding of the Holy Table there,reliſhes of Popery*. Ther-fore, if it doe not ſo much as *reliſh of popery*,it can neither *advance* it,nor *Uſher it in*. And therefore this is a moſt odious *ſlaunder*,and *ſcandall* caſt upon *Us*.

So here's *enough* both for the *Pra-ctiſe and Rule* of the Church of *Eng-land* ſince the *Reformation*. Now *before* that time, both in this and o-ther *Churches* of *Chriſtendome*,in the *Eaſt* and *Weſt ordinarily* the *Holy Ta-ble* or *Altar* ſtood *ſo*; Againſt this Mr. *Burton* ſayes little.

But the *Lincolne-Shire Miniſter* comes in to play the *Puritane* for that. Concerning which *Book* (fal-ling thus in my way) and the

Namelesse Author of it, I shall only say these *two things*.

The *one* is, that the *Author prevari-
cates* from the *first* word to the *last*
in the book, for he takes on him both
for the *Name* and for the *placing* of
the *Holy Table*, and the like, to prove,
that *Generally* and *Vniverfally*, and
Ordinarily in the whole *Catholicke
Church*, both *East* and *West*, the *Holy
Table* did not stand at the *upper* end
of the *Quire* or *Chancell*. And this
hee must *prove*, or he doth nothing.

Now when hee comes to make
his *Proofes*, they are almost *all* of
them *particular, few* or *none generall*
and *concludent*; For hee neither
brings *Testimonies* out of the *Generall* and received *Rituals* of the *Ea-
sterne* and *Westerne Churches*, nor of
Fathers and *Histories* of the *Church*,
which

which fpeake in *Generall* termes of
all, but where they fpeak of *particu-*
lar Churches only.

So that *fuppofe* the moft that can
be, that is, fuppofe his *quotations* bee
all *truly* alledged, and true too in the
fenfe that the *Minifter* takes them
(though in *very truth,* the *places, moft*
of them, are nei her *truly alledged,* nor
fenfed,) yet they are but *exceptions* of,
and *exemptions* fi om the *Gen rall*
practife. And you know both in *Law*
and *Reafon, Exceptio firmat Regulam*
in non exceptis. So that upon the fud-
den I am not able to *refolve,* whether
this *Minifter* hath done more *wrong*
to *himfelfe* or his *Readers,* for he hath
abufed both.

The *other* is, that in the *judgement*
of very *many learned* men, which
have perufed this book, the *Author*
is

is clearely conceived to *want* a great deale of that *learning* to which hee *pretends*: or elfe to have *written* this *Book wholly*, and R*efolvedly* againſt both his *ſcience* and his *conſcience*.

And for *my owne part*, I am *fully* of *opinion*, this *Booke* was *thruſt* now to the *Preſſe*, both to *countenance* theſe *Libellers*, and as much as in him lay, to *fire* both *Church* and *State*.

And though I *wonder not* at the *Miniſter*, yet I ſhould *wonder* at the *Biſhop* of the *Dioceſſe* (a man of lear-ning and experience)that he ſhould give *Teſtimony* to ſuch a *buſineſſe*, and in ſuch *times* as theſe.

And *once more*, before I leave the *Holy Table, Name, and Thing*, give me leave to put you in minde, that there is *no danger* at *all* in the *Altar, Name, or Thing*. For at the *begin-ning nmg* of the *Reformation*, though there were *a Law* for the taking downe of the *Altars*, and setting up of *Holy Tables* in the *roome* of them; yet in some places the *Altars* were *not suddenly removed*. And what sayes the *Queene* in her *Injunction* to this ? VVhy she sayes, *That there seemes no matter of great moment in this, saving for uniformity, and the better imitation of the Law in that behalfe.* Therefore for any *danger* or *hurt* that was in the *Altars, Name, or Thing,* they might *even then* have beene *left standing, but for Uniformity, and the Imitation of the Law.*

But howsoever, it followes in the same *Injunction, that when the* Altar *is taken downe, the Holy Table* shall *bee set* In, (*not* crosse) *the place where the Altar stood;* which (as is aforesaid) must

Injunct. ultim.

muſt needs be *Altar-wiſe*.

14. The *Fourteenth* and the *laſt Innovation* comes with a *mighty Charge*, & 'tis taken out of an *Epiſtle* to the *Temporall Lords* of his *Majeſties Privy Councell*. Of which *Epiſtle* we got one *ſheet*, and ſo (for ought I yet know) that *Impreſſion* ſtay'd : In that *Sheet* is this *charge*, The *words* are,

 The Prelates, to juſtifie their proceedings, have forged a new Article of Religion, brought from Rome *(which gives them full power to alter the Doctrine and Diſcipline of our Church at a Blow, as they Interpret it) and have foiſted it (* ſuch is their language *) into the beginning of the Twentieth Article of our* Church. And *this is in the laſt edition of the Articles,* Anno 1628. *in affront of his Majeſties Declaration before them,* &c. The

The *Clauſe* (which they ſay is *for-ged* by us) is this : *The Church,* (*that is, the Biſhops, as they expound it*) *hath power to decree Rites and Cere-monies, and Authority in matters of Faith.* (The *word* is *Controverſies* of *Faith,* by their leave) *This Clauſe* (ſay they) *is a forgery fit to be exami-ned, and deeply cenſured in the Star-chamber. For 'tis not to be found in the Latine or Engliſh Articles of* Edw. 6. or Q. Elizabeth, *ratified by Par-liament.*

And then in the margent thus, *If to forge a Will or Writing be cenſu-rable in the Star-chamber, which is but a wrong to a private man : How much more the forgery of an Article of Reli-gion, to wrong the whole Church, and overturne Religion which concernes all our ſoules.*

K   This

This is a *heavie charge, my Lords:*
But I thank G o d the *Anfwer's* eafie.

And *truly* I grant, that to *forge* an
Article of *Religion* in *whole* or in *part,*
and then to *thruft* it upon the *Church,*
is a moft *haynous crime,* farre worfe
then the *forging of a Deed.* And is
certainly *very deeply cenfurable* in this
Court. And I would have humbly
befought you, that a *deepe cenfure*
might have beene layd upon *it,* but
that this *fheet* was found after, and fo
is not annexed to the *Information,*
nor in *Iudgement* at this *prefent* before you.

But then, *My Lords,* I muft tell
you, I hope to make it as *cleere* as the
day, that this *forgery* was not, *that*
this *claufe* mentioned was added, by
the *Prelates* to the *Article,* to gaine
power to the *Church,* and fo to ferve
our

our turnes. But that that *clause* in the *beginning* of the *Article* was by these men, or at least by some of their *Faction, razed out,* and this to weaken the *just* power of the *Church* to serve *their turnes.*

They say (to *justifie* their *charge*) that this *clause* is not to be found in the *Articles, English* or *Latine,* of either *Ed.6.* or Q. *Elizabeth.*

I answer: The *Articles* of *Edw.6.* and those made under Q. *Elizabeth* *differ* very much. And those of *Ed. 6.* are not now *binding.* So whether the *Clause* be *in* or *out* of *them,* 'tis not much *materiall.*

But for the *Articles* of the *Church* of *England,* made in the Queenes time, and now in *force,* that this *clause* for the *power* of the *Church* to *decree Ceremonies, and to have Authority in con-*

troversies

troverfies of faith, ſhold not be found in *Engliſh* or *Latine Copies*, till the *Yeare*, 1628. that it was ſet forth with the *Kings Declaration* before it, is to me a *miracle*; but *your Lordſhips* ſhall ſee the *falſehood* and *boldnes* of theſe men.

What? Is this *affirmative clauſe* in no *Copie*, *Engliſh* or *Latine* till the *Yeare* 1628 ? *Strange:* VVhy, my *Lords*, I have a *Copie* of the *Articles* in *Engliſh*, of the *Yeare*, 1612. And of the *Yeare*, 1605. and of the *Yeare*, 1593 and in *Latine* of the *Yeare*, 1563. which was one of the *firſt printed Co-pies*, if not the *firſt of all*. For the Ar-ticles were *agreed* on but the *Nine and twentieth day of January,* *Anno* 156 $\begin{cases} 2. \\ 3. \end{cases}$ According to the *Engliſh* Account. According to the *Iulian* Account.

And in all theſe, this *Affirmative Clauſe* for the Churches *power* is *in*.

And

And is not this ſtrange *boldnes* then to *abuſe* the VVorld, and falſely to ſay 'tis in no *Copie*, when *J my ſelfe*, out of my own *ſtore*, am able to ſhew it in ſo *many*, and ſo *aunciently*.

But *My Lords*, I ſhall make it plainer yet: For 'tis not fit concer- ning an *Article* of *Religion*, and an *Article* of ſuch *conſequence* for the *Order*, *Truth*, and *Peace* of this *Church*, you ſhould *rely* upon my *Co- pies*, be they never ſo *many* or never ſo *auncient*.

Therefore I ſent to the *Publike Records* in my *Office*, and here un- der my *Officers* hand, who is a *Pub- like Notary*, is returned mee the *Twentieth Article* with this *Affir- matiue Clauſe* in it. And there is alſo the whole *Body* of the *Articles* to be ſeene.

K 3   By

By this your *Lordſhips* ſee how free the *Prelates* are from *forging* this part of the *Article.* Now let theſe men quit themſelves and their *faction,* as they can, for their *Index Expurgatorius* and their foule *Raſure* in leaving out this *part* of the *Article.* For to *leave out* of an *Article* is as great a *Crime* as to *put in;* And a *Maine Raſure* is as *cenſurable* in this *Court* as a *forgery.*

Why, but then my *Lords;* what is this *Myſtery of Iniquity?*

Truly, I cannot certainely tell, but as farre as I can, I'le tell you.

The *Articles* you ſee were *fully,* and *fairely* agreed to, and *ſubſcribed* in the *yeare*---156$\frac{2}{3}$. But after this, in the *yeare* 1571. there were ſome that *refuſed* to *ſubſcribe,* but why they did ſo is not *recorded.* Whether

ther it were about this *Article* or
any other I know not. But in fact
this is manifeft, that in that *yeare*
1571. the *Articles* were *printed* both
in *Latine*, and *Englifh*, and this
Claufe for the *Church* left out of both.
And certainely, this could not bee
done, but by the *malicious cunning*
of that *Oppofite Faction*. And
though I fhall fpare *dead* mens
names where I have not *certainty*;
Yet if you bee *pleafed* to *looke backe*
and *confider* who they were that
Governed bufineffes in 1571, and
rid the Church almoft at their *plea-*
fure; And how *potent* the *Anceftors*,
thefe *Libellers* began *then* to *growe*,
you will thinke it no *hard* matter to
have the *Articles printed*, and *this*
Claufe left out.
    And yet 'tis plaine, That, after
                         the

the ftirre about *Subfcription* in the
yeare 1571. the *Articles* were *fetled*
and *fubfcribed* unto at laft, as in the
yeare 1562. with this *Claufe* in them
for the Church : For looking farther into the *Records* which are in
mine own hands, I have found the
Booke of 156⅔ fubfcribed by *all* the
Lower houfe of Convocation, in this
very *yeare* of *Contradiction*, 1571. Dr.
Iohn Elmar (who was after *Lord
Bifhop of London*) being there *Pro-
loquutor* : *Alexander Nowell Deane
of Saint Pauls*, having beene *Pro-
loquutor* in 156⅔ and yet living and
prefent and fubfcribing in, 1571.
Therefore, I doe here openly in
Star-chamber charge upon that *pure
Sect* this *foule corruption* of *falfify-
ing the Articles* of the Church of
England, let them take it off as they
can.   I

I have now done, and 'tis time
I should, with the *Innovations*
charded upon the *Prelates,* and fit
to be answered here.

Some few more there are, but
they belong to matter of *Doctrine,*
which shall presently be answered,
Iusto Volumine, at large, to *satisfie* all
wel-minded people. But when Mr.
Burtons Booke, which is the *maine*
one, is *answered,* (I meane his *Booke,*
not his *Rayling*) neither *Prynne,*
nor *Bastwicke ,* nor any *Attendants*
upon *Rabshakeh* shall *by me* or *my
care* be *answered.* If this *Court* find not
a way to *stop* these *Libellers mouthes*
and *pennes,* for *me* they shall *rayle*
on till they be *weary*

Yet *one* thing more I beseech
you, give *Me* leave to *adde.* 'Tis
Master *Burtons charge* * upon the *Pag* 175.
L   *Prelates*

Prelates. That the Cenſures formerly laid upon Malefaƈtors, are now put upon Gods Miniſters for their Vertue and Piety.

A *heavy charge* this too. But if he or *any man* elſe can *ſhew* that any man hath been *puniſhed* in the *High Commiſſion,* or elſe where, by the *Prelates,* for *Vertue* and *Piety,* there is all the reaſon in the world *we* ſhould bee *ſeverely puniſhed* our ſelves. But the truth is, the *Vertue* and *Piety* for which theſe *Miniſters* are *puniſhed,* is for preaching *Schiſme* and *ſedition,* many of their *Sermons* being as bad as their *Libels;* As *Burtons Libell* was one of his *Sermons* firſt. But whether this ſtuffe have any *Affinity* with *Vertue* and *Piety,* I ſubmit to any *Chriſtian Reader.*

And

And yet Mr. *Burton* is so *confident*
of his *Innocency*, even in *this cause*
wherein hee hath so *fouly* carryed
himselfe, that hee breakes forth into
these words*, *I never so much as once*   * *Pag.7.*
dreamed, that Impiety and Impudency
it selfe in such a Christian State as this
is, and under such a gracious Prince ,
durst ever thus publikely have called me
in question, and that upon the open
Stage, &c.

You see the *boldnesse* of the *Man*,
and in as *bad a Cause*, as (I think) in
this kind ever *any man* had.

I shall *end* all with a passage out
of *S. Cyprian,* 'when he, then *Bishop*   f *Lib.1.*
of *Carthage,* was *bitterly rayled* upon   *Ep. 3.*
by a pack of *Schifmaticks, his answer*
was, and 'tis now *mine;* They have
rayled both *bitterly* and *falsly* upon

me, and yet *Non oportet me paria cum illis facere;* it becomes not *me* to an-ſwer them with the like, either *Levities* or *Revilings,* but to *ſpeake* and *write* that only which becomes *Sacerdotem Dei,* a *Prieſt* of Go d.

Neither ſhall I in this *give way* (though I have beene *extreamly* vilified) to either *griefe* or *paſsion* to *ſpeak, remembring* that of the *Pſal-*

a Pſal.37.8. *miſt* a *Pſal.* 37. *Fret not thy ſelfe, elſe ſhalt thou be moved to do evill.*

Neither yet by *Gods grace* ſhall the *Reproaches* of *ſuch* men as *theſe,* make me *faint* or *ſtart aſide,* either from the *Right way* in matter of *pra-Ɐiſe* (they are *S. Cyprians* words

* Ib.p.10. againe *) or *à certâ regulâ,* from the certaine rule of *faith.*

And ſince in *former* times, ſome

ſpared

ſpared not to call the *Maſter* of the houſe *Beelʒebub*, how much more will they bee *bold* with *them* of his *houſhold*, as it is in S. *Matthew* *, *Chap.* 10. And ſo *bold* have theſe men been; but the next *words* of our *Saviour* are, *Feare them not.*

*S. *Mat.* 10. 25.

I humbly crave *pardon* of your *Lordſhips* for this my *neceſſary length*, and give you *all* hearty thankes for your *Noble patience,* and your *Juſt and Honourable cenſure* upon theſe Men, and your *Vnanimous diſlike* of them, and *defence* of the *Church*.

But becauſe the *buſineſſe* hath ſome *reflection* upon *my ſelfe*, I ſhall *forbeare* to *cenſure* them, and *leave* them to GODS *mercy,* and the KINGS *juſtice.*

FINIS.